A Playful Palett
10 KNITTED
ACCESSORIES™

Tabetha Hedrick

Annie's®

MW00559075

Introduction

. . . .

There's something wonderfully soothing about knitting accessories. I don't know whether it is the portability, the simplicity of construction or the instant gratification aspect, but accessories are just the ticket for a comforting knitting experience.

These pieces were inspired by the concept of travel (and are thusly named after various airports) in all forms: easy to carry and work on throughout any form of transportation, quick to knit and perfect for that sensation of feeling trendy when you step off a plane.

The designs are customizable, loaded with simple texture and entertaining for all levels of knitters. From sassy scarves to squishy socks, capes for layering and mitts for cool weather, you will find everything you need for the perfect knitwear indulgence.

Tabetha

A Playful Palette of 10 Knitted Accessories

Table of Contents

Kodiak Cowl,
page 15

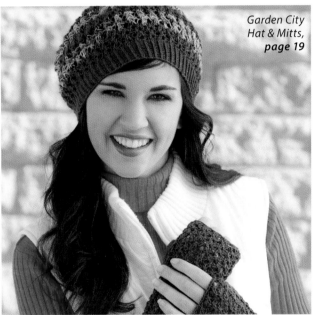

Garden City
Hat & Mitts,
page 19

Hilo Scarflette,
page 29

Nantucket Socks,
page 36

Day Tripper

Sassy in a flash, you're a trendsetter without even trying. Whether you are styling on the beach or preparing for a night on the town, each piece is cute, deliciously simple and super hip. The bonus? You'll be chic in less than 85 yards.

Friday Harbor Headband

When I'm on the road to warmer weather, especially down south, I just want my hair out of the way so that it doesn't stick to my skin. Funky cables and bright pops of color make perfect sense to me in a headband! The best part is that you can use your leftover scrap yarn to whip out this lovely, portable project.

. . . .

Skill Level

■■■□ INTERMEDIATE

Finished Measurements
Width: 2¼ inches
Length: Adjustable to fit

Materials
- Koigu KPM (fingering weight; 100% merino wool; 175 yds/50g per skein): 75 yds pink #1170 (sample used leftover yarn from Kodiak Braided Cowl on page 15)
- Size 4 (3.5mm) needles or size needed to obtain gauge
- Size E/4 (3.5mm) crochet hook
- Cable needle

Gauge
36 sts and 36 rows = 4 inches/10cm in Cable pat.

Exact gauge is not critical for this project.

Special Abbreviations
2 over 2 Right Cross (2/2 RC): Slip 2 sts to cn and hold in back; k2, k2 from cn.

2 over 2 Right Purl Cross (2/2 RPC): Slip 2 sts to cn and hold in back; k2, p2 from cn.

2 over 2 Left Cross (2/2 LC): Slip 2 sts to cn and hold in front; k2, k2 from cn.

2 over 2 Left Purl Cross (2/2 LPC): Slip 2 sts to cn and hold in front; p2, k2 from cn.

Pattern Stitches
Seed St (3 sts)
Row 1: K1, p1, k1.
Rep Row 1 for pat.

Cable (14-st panel)

Note: A chart is provided for those preferring to work pat st from a chart.

Row 1 (RS): K2, [p2, k2] twice, 2/2 RC.
Row 2 and all WS rows: Work all sts as they present themselves (knit the knit sts and purl the purl sts).
Row 3: [K2, p2] twice, 2/2 RPC, k2.
Row 5: K2, p2, k2, 2/2 RC, p2, k2.
Row 7: K2, 2/2 RPC, k2, p2, k2.
Row 9: K2, 2/2 RC, [p2, k2] twice.
Row 11: 2/2 RPC, k2, [p2, k2] twice.
Rows 13–24: Rep Rows 1–12.
Row 25: 2/2 LC, k2, [p2, k2] twice.
Row 27: K2, 2/2 LPC, [p2, k2] twice.
Row 29: K2, p2, 2/2 LC, k2, p2, k2.
Row 31: K2, p2, k2, 2/2 LPC, p2, k2.
Row 33: [K2, p2] twice, 2/2 LC, k2.
Row 35: K2, [p2, k2] twice, 2/2 LPC.
Rows 37–48: Rep Rows 25–36.
Rep Rows 1–48 for pat.

Headband
Using a provisional cast-on (see page 46), cast on 20 sts.

Set-up row (WS): Work 3 sts in Seed St; k2, p2, [k2, p2] twice, k2; work 3 sts in Seed St.

Maintaining first and last 3 sts in Seed St, work 48-row Cable pat until piece measures approx 1–2 inches shorter than your head circumference, ending with a WS row.

Finishing
Unzip provisional cast-on and place live sts on separate needle.

Graft the ends tog using Kitchener st (see page 46) for St st.

Block lightly. Weave in ends. ●

STITCH KEY

☐	K on RS, p on WS
−	P on RS, k on WS
⤬	2/2 LC
⤬	2/2 LPC
⤬	2/2 RC
⤬	2/2 RPC

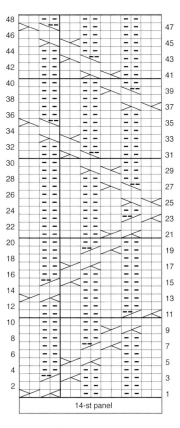

CABLE CHART

Del Rio Bangles

Worked in a flash with scraps of leftover yarns, these bangles are exactly what you're looking for. You'll be thrilled with the results of this ridiculously easy pattern!

. . . .

Skill Level
■■□□□ EASY

Finished Measurement
Circumference: 10 inches

Materials
- Koigu KPM (fingering weight; 100% merino wool; 175 yds/50g per skein): 25 yds purple #2169 or blue #2173 (sample used leftover yarn from Kodiak Braided Cowl on page 15)
- Size 7 (4.5mm) needles or size needed to obtain gauge
- 10-inch-circumference, 2-inch-wide plastic bangle for each bracelet

1 SUPER FINE

Gauge
16 sts and 37 rows = 4 inches/10cm in Fisherman's Rib.

To save time, take time to check gauge.

Special Abbreviation
Knit 1 Below (k1B): Insert needle into center of st in row below the next st and k1.

Pattern Stitch
Fisherman's Rib (multiple of 2 sts + 2)
All rows: K1, [k1B, k1] to last st, k1.

Bracelet
With color of choice, cast on 40 sts.

Work in Fisherman's Rib until piece measures 2½ inches.

Bind off loosely.

Finishing
Block lightly.

Sew side seam.

Weave in ends.

Place over bangle and sew bound-off edge to cast-on edge, wrapping around the bracelet as you go. •

Jet-Setter

Bold, rich colors of tangerine, blue and fuchsia make you stand out in the crowd. You hopped off that plane ready to make a statement, to strut your stuff. These pieces, loaded with sultry lace and beautiful simplicity, will get you there.

Bethel

This scarf is worked on the bias, which means that it resembles a parallelogram. Knit with one skein, it is quickly finished in a couple of hours! In fact, my own sample was knit on the 2½ hour flight between Denver and Columbus. With its luxurious lace pattern and deliciously long length, you'll delight in experimenting with the many different ways to wear it!

Skill Level

 EASY

Finished Measurements
Approx 4¾ inches wide x 107 inches long

Materials
*   Koigu KPPPM (fingering-weight yarn; 100% merino wool, 175 yds/50g per skein): 1 skein orange hand-paint #P908 or Koigu KPM solid orange/ yellow #1240

1 SUPER FINE

*   Size 11 (8mm) needles or size needed to obtain gauge

Gauge
16 sts and 17 rows = 4 inches/10cm in Lace pat, blocked.

Exact gauge is not critical for this project.

Pattern Note
A chart is provided for the scarf pattern for those preferring to work the pattern from a chart.

Scarf
With color of choice, cast on 19 sts.

Set-up row (WS): K1, purl to last 2 sts, p2tog— 18 sts.

Row 1 (RS): K1, [k3, yo, k3tog, yo] twice, k4, kfb— 19 sts.

Rows 2 and 4 (WS): K1, purl to last 2 sts, p2tog— 18 sts.

Row 3: K3, [k3, yo, k3tog, yo] twice, k2, kfb—19 sts.

Row 5: K2, yo, k3tog, yo, [k3, yo, k3tog, yo] twice, kfb—19 sts.

Row 6: Rep Row 2.

Rep Rows 1–6 until scarf measures a finished length of 107 inches or desired length, ending with a WS row.

Bind off loosely on next RS row.

Finishing
Block scarf to finished measurements. Weave in ends.

Tie as shown in Fig 1 or as desired. ●

FIGURE 1

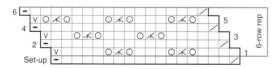

SCARF CHART

STITCH KEY

☐	K on RS, p on WS
−	K on WS
○	Yo
⟋	K3tog
V	Kfb
⟋	P2tog on WS

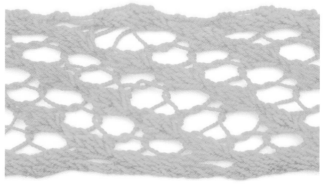

Kodiak Cowl

Cowls are one of the most fun, yet simple, knitwear projects out there. You'll look like a jet-setter just stepping off a plane from New York with this easy-to-work cowl. Lace strips braided together create a wealth of texture that catches the eye.

. . . .

Skill Level
■■■□ INTERMEDIATE

Finished Measurement
Circumference: 30 inches, braided

Materials
- Koigu KPM (fingering weight; 100% merino wool, 175 yds/50g per skein): 1 skein each blue #2173 (A), pink #1170 (B), and purple #2169 (C)
- Size 7 (4.5mm) needles or size needed to obtain gauge
- Spare set of size 7 needles
- Size H/8 (5mm) crochet hook

1 SUPER FINE

Gauge
17 sts and 21 rows = 4 inches/10cm in Lace pat (blocked).

Exact gauge is not critical for this project.

Pattern Stitch
Lace (multiple of 2 sts + 2)

Row 1 (RS): K1, [yo, k2tog] 8 times, k1.
Row 2 (WS): K1, purl to last st, k1.
Row 3: K1, [k2tog, yo] 8 times, k1.
Row 4: K1, purl to last st, k1.
Rep Rows 1–4 for pat.

Pattern Note
The cowl is constructed as follows: Work 1 strip in each of 3 colors. Join the 3 cast-on ends, braid the strips, join the remaining 3 ends, and then graft the joined ends together to form cowl.

Cowl
Make 3 Strips

Using provisional cast-on (see page 46) and A, cast on 18 sts.

Row 1 (WS): K1, purl to last st, k1.

Work [4-row Lace pat] 27 times, or until piece measures desired length, ending with Row 1.

Transfer sts to holder and set aside.

Work 2 more strips in the same manner but using B and C.

Finishing
Block as desired.

Unzip the provisional cast-on edges and **transfer live sts of each strip to separate needles. Layer the 3 strips so that the WS of each is facing you and all needles are pointing to the right.

Join the ends as follows: With WS facing, *purl first st of each strip tog; rep from * across.**

Transfer sts to holder.

Braid the 3 strips loosely.

Rep from ** to ** to join ends.

Transfer joined sts at other end to separate needle.

Graft the beg and end of braid using Kitchener st (see page 46).

Weave in ends. ●

Garden City Hat & Mitts

Slouch hats are stylish, comfortable and keep your hair tame while traveling across the globe. This hat, along with the ultra-sleek fingerless mitts, combines texture, color and lace to achieve a beautiful result.

. . . .

Skill Level
■■■□ INTERMEDIATE

Hat
Sizes
Woman's small (medium, large)

Instructions given are for smallest size, with larger sizes in parentheses. When only 1 number is given, it applies to all sizes.

Finished Measurement
Circumference: 18½ (19½, 21) inches

Materials
- Koigu KPM (fingering weight; 100% merino wool; 175 yds/50g per skein): 1 skein teal #1500 (A)
- Koigu KPPPM (fingering weight; 100% merino wool; 175 yds/50g per skein): 1 skein pink/black/teal #P153 (B)
- Size 4 (3.5mm) 16-inch circular needle or size needed to obtain gauge
- Size 5 (3.75mm) 16-inch circular and double-point needles (set of 5) or size needed to obtain gauge
- Stitch markers, 1 in CC for beg of rnd

Hat
Gauge
26 sts and 40 rnds = 4 inches/10cm in Twisted Rib with smaller needle.

20 sts and 26 rnds = 4 inches/10cm in Lace pat with larger needle.

To save time, take time to check gauge.

Pattern Stitches
Twisted Rib (even number of sts)
Every rnd: *[K1-tbl, p1; rep from * around.

Lace (multiple of 3 sts)
Rnd 1: *K2, p1; rep from * around.
Rnd 2: *Yo, ssk, p1; rep from * around
Rnd 3: *K2, p1; rep from * around.
Rnd 4: *K2tog, yo, p1; rep from * around.
Rep Rnds 1–4 for pat.

Open Lace (multiple of 6 sts)
Rnd 1: *Yo, k3tog, yo, k3; rep from * around.
Rnd 2: *K3, yo, k3tog, yo; rep from * around.
Rep Rnds 1 and 2 for pat.

Pattern Notes
Circumference is based on Twisted Rib.

When shaping crown in Lace pattern, if you cannot work both the yarn over and its accompanying decrease, work in stockinette stitch.

Hat

Body

With A and smaller needle, cast on 120 (126, 132) sts; pm for beg of rnd and join, taking care not to twist sts.

Work 10 rnds in Twisted Rib.

Change to larger needle.

*With A, work [4-rnd Lace pat] twice.

Change to B; knit 1 rnd.

Work [2-rnd Open Lace pat] 4 times.

Rep from * twice more. Cut B.

With A, work 4-rnd Lace pat until piece measures approx 9 (9½, 10) inches or desired length to crown, slightly stretched.

Shape Crown

Note: Change to dpns when sts no longer fit comfortably on circular needle.

Set-up rnd: *Work 12 (14, 12) sts in Lace pat, pm; rep from * around.

Dec rnd: *Work in pat to 2 sts before marker, k2tog; rep from * around—110 (117, 121) sts.

Rep Dec rnd [every rnd] 10 (12, 10) more times—10 (9, 11) sts.

Next rnd: [K2tog] 5 (4, 5) times, k0 (1, 1)—5 (5, 6) sts.

Cut yarn, leaving a 5-inch tail.

Using tapestry needle, thread tail through rem sts, pull tight and secure end.

Finishing

Weave in all ends.

Block as desired.

T!P

To make your hat look even lacier, work double yarn overs, and on the following rounds drop one of the yarn overs and knit into the single long loop.

Skill Level

 INTERMEDIATE

Mitts
Sizes
Woman's small/medium (large/X-large)

Instructions given are for smallest size, with larger sizes in parentheses. When only 1 number is given, it applies to both sizes.

Finished Measurements:
Circumference: 7 (8½) inches
Length: 8 (9) inches

Materials
- Koigu KPM (fingering weight; 100% merino wool; 175 yds/50g per skein): 1 skein teal #1500 (A)
- Size 5 (3.75mm) double-point needles (set of 5) or size needed to obtain gauge
- Stitch markers

Mitts

Gauge
20 sts and 26 rnds = 4 inches/10cm in Lace pat.

To save time, take time to check gauge.

Special Abbreviations
Make 1 Left (M1L): Insert LH needle from front to back under strand between sts; knit into back of resulting loop.

Make 1 Right (M1R): Insert LH needle from back to front under strand between sts; knit into front of resulting loop.

Pattern Stitches
Twisted Rib (even number of sts)
Every rnd: *K1-tbl, p1; rep from * around.

Lace (multiple of 3 sts)
Rnd 1: *K2, p1; rep from * around.
Rnd 2: *Yo, ssk, p1; rep from * around
Rnd 3: *K2, p1; rep from * around.
Rnd 4: *K2tog, yo, p1; rep from * around.
Rep Rnds 1–4 for pat.

Special Technique
Twisted German Cast-On

Set-up: Leaving a long tail, make a slip knot and put it on a needle. Place the thumb and index finger of your left hand between the yarn ends, with the long yarn tail over your thumb and the strand from the skein over your index finger. Close your other fingers over the strands to hold them against your palm. Spread your thumb and index fingers apart and draw the yarn into a "V."

Step 1: Bring the needle in front of the strands around thumb.

Step 2: Take the needle under both strands on thumb and then down through the loop formed by the thumb strands.

Step 3: Go over the top of the front strand on the index finger, and then scoop under to catch the strand.

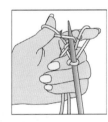

Step 4: Take the needle down through the loop on thumb, bending/twisting the thumb to untwist the loop and allow the needle to go through.

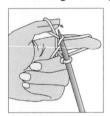

Step 5: Drop the loop from your thumb and draw up the strand to form a stitch on the needle. Put your hand back in the "V" position.

Repeat Steps 1–5 until you have cast on the number of stitches indicated in the pattern. Remember to count the beginning slip knot as a stitch. Watch the video for this cast-on here: AnniesCatalog.com/detail.html?prod_id=105514

Mitts

Lower Hand

Using Twisted German Cast-On or your favorite stretchy cast-on technique, cast on 36 (42) sts; mark beg of rnd and join, taking care not to twist sts.

Work 4 rnds Twisted Rib pat.

Change to Lace pat; work even until mitt measures 4½ (5) inches or to desired length.

Thumb Gusset

Rnd 1 (set-up): Work 18 (21) sts in pat, pm, M1L, pm, work 18 (21) sts to end of rnd—1 gusset st.

Rnd 2 (inc): Maintaining Lace pat outside of markers, work to marker, slip marker, M1R, k1-tbl, M1L, slip marker, work in pat to end of rnd— 3 gusset sts.

Rnd 3: Work to marker, slip marker, p1, k1-tbl, p1, slip marker, work to end of rnd.

Rnd 4 (inc): Work to marker, slip marker, M1R, p1, k1-tbl, p1, M1L, slip marker, work to end of rnd—5 gusset sts.

Rnds 5 and 6: Work to marker, [k1-tbl, p1] twice, k1-tbl, work to end of rnd.

Maintaining Lace pat outside of markers, continue to inc 1 at each side of gusset on next rnd, then [inc 1 at each side every 3 rnds] 4 (6) more times, working new gusset sts into established Twisted Rib pat—15 (17) gusset sts.

Upper Hand

Next rnd: Removing gusset markers when you come to them, work to marker, work Twisted Rib pat to next marker; turn so that the WS of the thumb gusset is facing you, bind off 15 (17) gusset sts in pat, turn, slip last st from bind-off to RH needle; continue working Lace pat to end of rnd—36 (42) sts.

Work even until mitt measures 2 inches from thumb gusset bind-off row or to desired length, ending on Rnd 2 or 4.

Bind off loosely in pat.

Finishing

Weave in ends.

Block as desired. •

For a less slouchy version of
this whimsical cap, create this
one-skein alternative.

Skill Level
 INTERMEDIATE

Sizes
Woman's small (medium, large)

Instructions given are for smallest size, with larger sizes in parentheses. When only 1 number is given, it applies to all sizes.

Finished Measurement
Circumference: 18½ (19½, 21) inches

Materials
- Koigu KPPPM (fingering weight; 100% merino wool; 175 yds/50g per skein): 1 skein pink #P105
- Size 4 (3.5mm) 16-inch circular needle or size needed to obtain gauge
- Size 5 (3.75mm) 16-inch circular and double-point needles (set of 5) or size needed to obtain gauge
- Stitch markers, 1 in CC for beg of rnd

Hat
Gauge
26 sts and 40 rnds = 4 inches/10cm in Twisted Rib with smaller needle.

20 sts and 26 rnds = 4 inches/10cm in Lace pat with larger needle.

To save time, take time to check gauge.

Pattern Stitches
Twisted Rib (even number of sts)
Every rnd: *K1-tbl, p1; rep from * around.

Lace (multiple of 3 sts)
Rnd 1: *K2, p1; rep from * around.
Rnd 2: *Yo, ssk, p1; rep from * around
Rnd 3: *K2, p1; rep from * around.
Rnd 4: *K2tog, yo, p1; rep from * around.
Rep Rnds 1–4 for pat.

Pattern Notes
Circumference is based on Twisted Rib.

When shaping crown in Lace pattern, if you cannot work both the yarn over and its accompanying decrease, work in stockinette stitch.

Hat
Body
With smaller needle, cast on 120 (126, 132) sts; pm for beg of rnd and join, taking care not to twist sts.

Work 10 rnds in Twisted Rib.

Change to larger needle.

Work even in Lace pat until piece measures approx 9 (9½, 10) inches or desired length to crown, slightly stretched.

Shape Crown
Note: Change to dpns when sts no longer fit comfortably on circular needle.

Set-up rnd: *Work 12 (14, 12) sts in Lace pat, pm; rep from * around.

Dec rnd: *Work in pat to 2 sts before marker, k2tog; rep from * around—110 (117, 121) sts.

Rep Dec rnd [every rnd] 10 (12, 10) more times—10 (9, 11) sts.

Next rnd: [K2tog] 5 (4, 5) times, k0 (1, 1)—5 (5, 6) sts.

Cut yarn, leaving a 5-inch tail.

Using tapestry needle, thread tail through rem sts, pull tight and secure end.

Finishing
Weave in all ends.

Block as desired. ●

Weekend Warrior

A luxurious weekend getaway is exactly what we need. Sumptuous, lavish and yet amazingly easy knits are just the ticket for that whole experience. With just a few skeins and a weekend squirreled away, you'll delight in the plush, comfortable and gorgeous results.

Hilo Scarflette

When traveling, don't you wish for a little something to wrap around your neck or shoulders? This charming piece, complete with ruffles and texture, fits the bill. Thick and rich with comfort, this two-stranded scarflette will delight your knitting senses.

. . . .

Skill Level

■■■□ INTERMEDIATE

Finished Measurements
8½ inches wide x 45½ inches long

Materials
- Koigu KPM (fingering weight; 100% merino wool; 175 yds/50g per skein): 3 skeins turquoise #2130 (A)
- Koigu KPPPM (fingering weight; 100% merino wool; 175 yds/50g per skein): 1 skein variegated turquoise #P743 (B)
- Size 8 (5mm) 24-inch circular needle or size needed to obtain gauge

1 SUPER FINE

Gauge
14 sts and 36 rows = 4 inches/10cm in Fisherman's Rib with 2 strands held tog.

Exact gauge is not critical for this project.

Special Abbreviations
Knit 1 Below (k1B): Insert needle into center of st below next st and k1.

Make 1 Left (M1L): Insert LH needle from front to back under strand between sts; knit into back of resulting loop.

Pattern Stitches
Fisherman's Rib (multiple of 2 sts + 2)
All Rows: K1, [k1B, k1] to last st, k1.

Short-Row Pat
Row 1 (RS): K1, [k1B, k1] 11 times, k1B, turn—6 sts rem unworked.
Row 2: K1, [k1B, k1] 11 times, k1.
Row 3: K1, [k1B, k1] 8 times, k1B, turn—12 sts rem unworked.
Row 4: K1, [k1B, k1] 8 times, k1.
Row 5: K1, [k1B, k1] 5 times, k1B, turn—18 sts rem unworked.

Row 6: K1, [k1B, k1] 5 times, k1.
Row 7: K1, [k1B, k1] twice, k1B, turn—24 sts rem unworked.
Row 8: K1, [k1B, k1] twice, k1.
Row 9: K1, [k1B, k1] to last st, k1.
Row 10: K1, [k1B, k1] to last st, k1.
Rep Rows 1–10 for pat.

Pattern Note
The scarf is worked from end to end, with the curved shape produced by short rows.

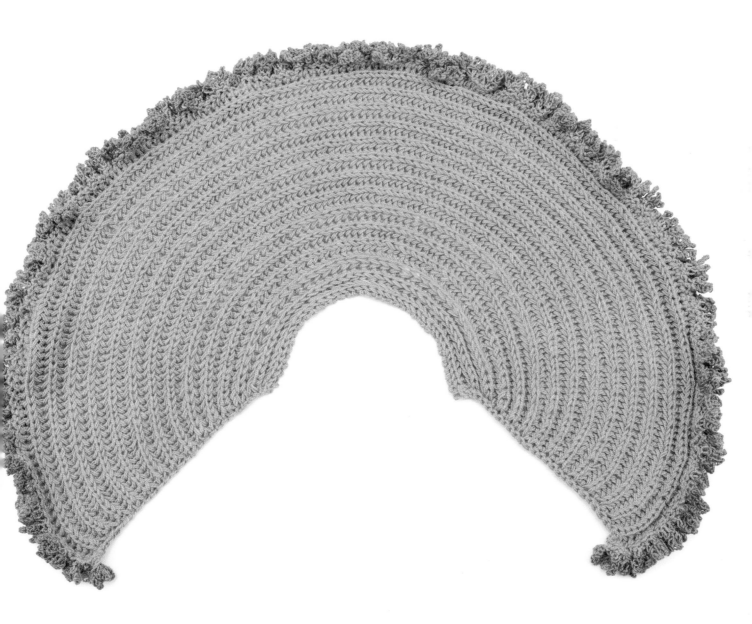

Scarf

Body

With 2 strands A held tog, cast on 30 sts.

Knit 1 WS row.

Work [10-row Short-Row Pat] 40 times or until scarf measures a finished length of 45 inches along the outside edge.

Bind off loosely.

Ruffled Edge

With RS facing and using 1 strand A, pick up and knit 1 st for every 2 rows across longest edge of scarf—200 sts.

Row 1 (WS): [Kfb] in each st across—400 sts.

Row 2 (RS): *K2, M1L; rep from * to last 2 sts, k2—599 sts. Cut A.

Mini-Fringe Bind-Off: Change to 1 strand B; *using cable method, cast on 4 sts, bind off 5 sts, pass st on RH needle back to LH needle; rep from * until all sts have been bound off.

Finishing

Weave in ends.

Block as desired. ●

Melbourne Cape

Drapey, loose and lovely, the Melbourne Cape highlights any wardrobe all year long. Layer it, wear it on an angle, or with the long or short edges at the front; the options are endless!

. . . .

Skill Level
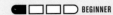 BEGINNER

Finished Measurements
Width: 51 inches
Length: 32 inches (16 inches when worn)

Materials
- Koigu KPPPM (fingering weight; 100% merino wool; 175 yds/50g per skein): 4 skeins light purple/green #P743
- Size 13 (9mm) 24-inch circular needle or size needed to obtain gauge

Gauge
11 sts and 17 rows = 4 inches/10cm in garter st (blocked).

Exact gauge is not critical for this project.

Pattern Note
Pattern is worked back and forth in rows. Circular needle is used to accommodate the large number of stitches. Do not join.

Cape
Cast on 140 sts.

Knit 68 rows, ending with a RS row.

Neck Opening
Row 1: K54, loosely bind off center 32 sts, knit to end.

Row 2: K54; using cable cast-on method (see page 44), cast on 32 sts; knit to end of row.

Knit 68 rows or until second half measures same as first half.

Bind off loosely.

Finishing
Weave in ends.

Block to measurements. ●

Nantucket Socks

Socks are the ultimate portable knitting project (and who doesn't love socks?) and indeed, you will love working these. A touch of soft lace and openwork lends the perfect amount of ease and comfort.

. . . .

Skill Level

 INTERMEDIATE

Sizes

Woman's small/medium (medium/large)

Instructions given are for smallest size, with larger size in parentheses. When only 1 number is given, it applies to both sizes.

Finished Measurements

Foot Circumference: 6¾ (9) inches
Foot Length: Adjustable to fit
Leg Length: 4½ or 8½ inches, as desired

Materials

- Koigu KPM (fingering weight; 100% merino wool; 175 yds/50g per skein): 2 skeins pink #2232 (short version) or turquoise #2130 (long version)
- Size 2 (2.75mm) double-point needles (set of 5) or size needed to obtain gauge

Gauge

28 sts and 40 rnds = 4 inches/10cm in St st.

28 sts and 36 rnds = 4 inches/10cm in Lace pat.

To save time, take time to check gauge.

Special Abbreviation

Wrap and Turn (W&T): Slip next st pwise to RH needle. Bring yarn to RS of work between needles, then slip same st back to LH needle. Bring yarn to WS, wrapping st. Turn, leaving rem sts unworked, then beg working back in the other direction. *To hide wraps on subsequent rows:* Work to wrapped st. With RH needle, pick up wrap and work wrap tog with wrapped st.

Pattern Stitch

Note: A chart is provided for those preferring to work pat st from a chart.

Lace (multiple of 16 sts)
Rnd 1: *[Ssk, yo] 3 times, k1, p1, yo, k2, ssk, k3, p1; rep from * around.
Rnd 2 and all even-number rnds: *[K7, p1] twice; rep from * around.
Rnd 3: *[Ssk, yo] 3 times, k1, p1, k1, yo, k2, ssk, k2, p1; rep from * around.
Rnd 5: *[Ssk, yo] 3 times, k1, p1, k2, yo, k2, ssk, k1, p1; rep from * around.
Rnd 7: *[Ssk, yo] 3 times, k1, p1, k3, yo, k2, ssk, p1; rep from * around.
Rnds 9–16: Rep Rnds 1–8.
Rnd 17: *K3, k2tog, k2, yo, p1, k1, [yo, k2tog] 3 times, p1; rep from * around.
Rnd 19: *K2, k2tog, k2, yo, k1, p1, k1, [yo, k2tog] 3 times, p1; rep from * around.

Rnd 21: *K1, k2tog, k2, yo, k2, p1, k1, [yo, k2tog] 3 times, p1; rep from * around.
Rnd 23: *K2tog, k2, yo, k3, p1, k1, [yo, k2tog] 3 times, p1; rep from * around.
Rnds 25–32: Rep Rnds 17–24.
Rep Rnds 1–32 for pat.

Pattern Notes

The leg is offered in two lengths, with the longer length in brackets.

This sock is worked from the cuff down with a short-row heel and a wedge toe.

Sock

Cuff

Cast on 48 (64) sts. Distribute sts evenly onto 4 dpns, 12 (16) on each; mark beg of rnd and join, taking care not to twist sts.

Work 16 rnds in 1x1 rib.

Leg

Change to Lace pat and work 32 [64] rnds.

Short-Row Heel

Transfer sts from 2nd dpn to first dpn for heel—24 (32) sts.

The rem sts are left on hold for instep.

Row 1 (RS): Knit to last heel st, W&T.

Row 2 (WS): Purl to last heel st, W&T.

Row 3: Knit to 1 st before last wrapped st, W&T.

Row 4: Purl to 1 st before last wrapped st, W&T.

Rep [last 2 rows] 5 (7) more times, ending with a WS row—10 (14) sts rem unwrapped at center of heel.

Row 1 (RS): K10 (14), knit wrapped st tog with its wrap, W&T. The st now has 2 wraps (double-wrapped).

Row 2 (WS): P11 (15), purl wrapped st tog with its wrap, W&T.

Row 3: Knit to double-wrapped st, knit st tog with its wraps, W&T.

Row 4: Purl to double-wrapped st, purl st tog with its wraps, W&T.

Rep last 2 rows until 1 double-wrapped st rem on each side.

Next rnd (RS): Knit to 1 st before double-wrapped st, knit st tog with its wraps. Continue around by working Lace pat across 24 (32) instep sts; continue around and work wrapped st tog with its wraps, then k11 (15) to center heel. Beg of rnd is now at center heel and sts are on 4 dpns.

Toe
Knit 1 rnd.

Dec rnd: *Knit to last 3 sts on first dpn, k2tog, k1;
k1, ssk, knit to end of 2nd dpn; rep from * on 3rd and 4th dpns—44 (60) sts.

Continuing in St st, rep Dec rnd [every other rnd] 5 more times—24 (40) sts.

Rep Dec rnd [every rnd] 2 (5) times—16 (20) sts.

K4 (5) sts to beg of instep. Cut yarn, leaving a 15-inch tail.

Graft instep and sole sts tog using Kitchener st (see page 46).

Finishing
Weave in ends.

Block as desired. ●

Foot
Work even in established pats (sole sts in St st and instep sts in Lace pat) until foot measures 1¼ (1¾) inches short of desired foot length, ending with an even-number rnd.

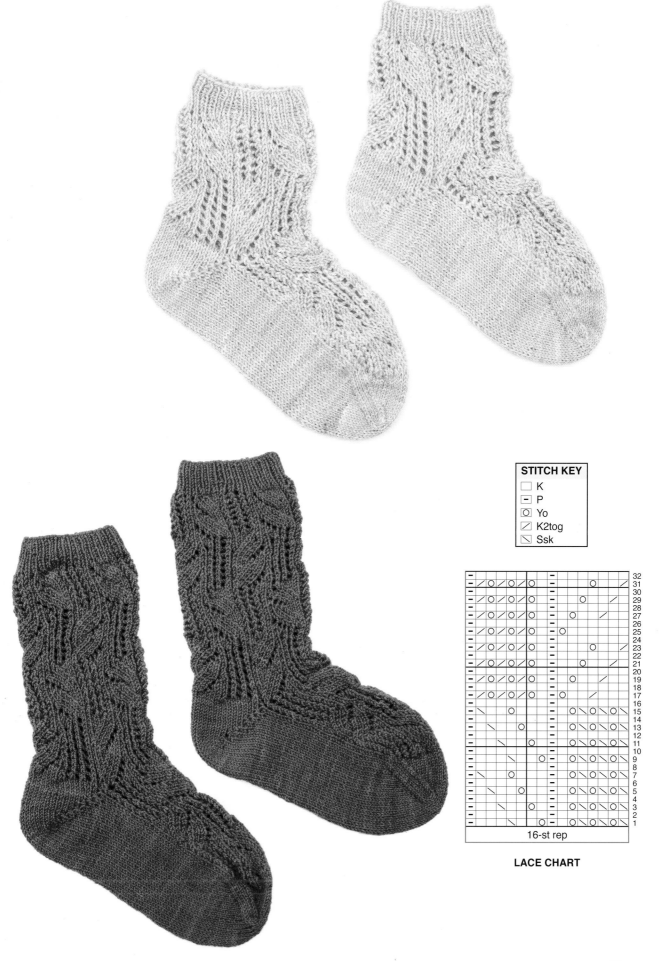

STITCH KEY

☐ K
⊟ P
▢ Yo
◪ K2tog
◩ Ssk

16-st rep

LACE CHART

General Information

Abbreviations & Symbols

[ ] work instructions within brackets as many times as directed

( ) work instructions within parentheses in the place directed

** repeat instructions following the asterisks as directed

* repeat instructions following the single asterisk as directed

" inch(es)

approx approximately
beg begin/begins/beginning
CC contrasting color
ch chain stitch
cm centimeter(s)
cn cable needle
dec(s) decrease/decreases/ decreasing
dpn(s) double-point needle(s)
g gram(s)
inc(s) increase/increases/ increasing

k knit
k2tog knit 2 stitches together
kfb knit in front and back
kwise knitwise
LH left hand
m meter(s)
M1 make one stitch
MC main color
mm millimeter(s)
oz ounce(s)
p purl
p2tog purl 2 stitches together
pat(s) pattern(s)
pm place marker
psso pass slipped stitch over
pwise purlwise
rem remain/remains/remaining
rep(s) repeat(s)
rev St st reverse stockinette stitch
RH right hand
rnd(s) rounds
RS right side

skp slip, knit, pass slipped stitch over—1 stitch decreased
sk2p slip 1, knit 2 together, pass slipped stitch over the knit 2 together—2 stitches decreased
sl slip
sl 1 kwise slip 1 knitwise
sl 1 pwise slip 1 purlwise
sl st slip stitch(es)
ssk slip, slip, knit these 2 stitches together—a decrease
st(s) stitch(es)
St st stockinette stitch
tbl through back loop(s)
tog together
WS wrong side
wyib with yarn in back
wyif with yarn in front
yd(s) yard(s)
yfwd yarn forward
yo (yo's) yarn over(s)

Skill Levels

BEGINNER

Beginner projects for first-time knitters using basic stitches. Minimal shaping.

EASY

Easy projects using basic stitches, repetitive stitch patterns, simple color changes and simple shaping and finishing.

INTERMEDIATE

Intermediate projects with a variety of stitches, mid-level shaping and finishing.

EXPERIENCED

Experienced projects using advanced techniques and stitches, detailed shaping and refined finishing.

Standard Yarn Weight System

Categories of yarn, gauge ranges and recommended needle sizes.

Yarn Weight Symbol & Category Names	0 LACE	1 SUPER FINE	2 FINE	3 LIGHT	4 MEDIUM	5 BULKY
Type of Yarns in Category	Fingering 10-Count Crochet Thread	Sock, Fingering, Baby	Sport, Baby	DK, Light Worsted	Worsted, Afghan, Aran	Chunky, Craft, Rug
Knit Gauge Range* in Stockinette Stitch to 4 inches	33–40 sts**	27–32 sts	23–26 sts	21–24 sts	16–20 sts	12–15 sts
Recommended Needle in Metric Size Range	1.5–2.25mm	2.25–3.25mm	3.25–3.75mm	3.75–4.5mm	4.5–5.5mm	5.5–8mm
Recommended Needle U.S. Size Range	000 to 1	1 to 3	3 to 5	5 to 7	7 to 9	9 to 11

* **GUIDELINES ONLY:** The above reflect the most commonly used gauges and needle sizes for specific yarn categories.

** Lace weight yarns are usually knitted on larger needles and hooks to create lacy, openwork patterns. Accordingly, a gauge range is difficult to determine. Always follow the gauge stated in your pattern.

Inches Into Millimeters & Centimeters

All measurements are rounded off slightly.

inches	mm	cm	inches	cm	inches	cm	inches	cm
⅛	3	0.3	5	12.5	21	53.5	38	96.5
¼	6	0.6	5½	14	22	56.0	39	99.0
⅜	10	1.0	6	15.0	23	58.5	40	101.5
½	13	1.3	7	18.0	24	61.0	41	104.0
⅝	15	1.5	8	20.5	25	63.5	42	106.5
¾	20	2.0	9	23.0	26	66.0	43	109.0
⅞	22	2.2	10	25.5	27	68.5	44	112.0
1	25	2.5	11	28.0	28	71.0	45	114.5
1¼	32	3.2	12	30.5	29	73.5	46	117.0
1½	38	3.8	13	33.0	30	76.0	47	119.5
1¾	45	4.5	14	35.5	31	79.0	48	122.0
2	50	5.0	15	38.0	32	81.5	49	124.5
2½	65	6.5	16	40.5	33	84.0	50	127.0
3	75	7.5	17	43.0	34	86.5		
3½	90	9.0	18	46.0	35	89.0		
4	100	10.0	19	48.5	36	91.5		
4½	115	11.5	20	51.0	37	94.0		

Knitting Basics

. . . .

Long-Tail Cast-On
Leaving an end about an inch long for each stitch to be cast on, make a slip knot on the right needle.

Place the thumb and index finger of your left hand between the yarn ends with the long yarn end over your thumb, and the strand from the skein over your index finger. Close your other fingers over the strands to hold them against your palm. Spread your thumb and index fingers apart and draw the yarn into a "V."

Place the needle in front of the strand around your thumb and bring it underneath this strand. Carry the needle over and under the strand on your index finger.

Draw through loop on thumb.

Drop the loop from your thumb and draw up the strand to form a stitch on the needle.

Repeat until you have cast on the number of stitches indicated in the pattern. Remember to count the beginning slip knot as a stitch.

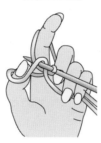

Cable Cast-On
This type of cast-on is used when adding stitches in the middle or at the end of a row.

Make a slip knot on the left needle. Knit a stitch in this knot and place it on the left needle. Insert the right needle between the last two stitches on the left needle. Knit a stitch and place it on the left needle. Repeat for each stitch needed.

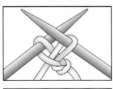

Knit (K)
Insert tip of right needle from front to back in next stitch on left needle.

Wrap yarn under and over the tip of the right needle.

Pull yarn loop through the stitch with right needle point.

Slide the stitch off the left needle. The new stitch is on the right needle.

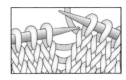

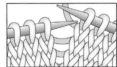

Purl (P)
With yarn in front, insert tip of right needle from back to front through next stitch on the left needle.

Wrap yarn around the right needle counterclockwise. With right needle, draw yarn back through the stitch.

Slide the stitch off the left needle.

The new stitch is on the right needle.

Invisible Increase (M1)
There are several ways to make or increase one stitch.

Make 1 With Left Twist (M1L)
Insert left needle from front to back under the horizontal loop between the last stitch worked and next stitch on left needle.

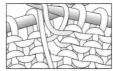

With right needle, knit into the back of this loop.

To make this increase on the purl side, insert left needle in same manner and purl into the back of the loop.

Make 1 With Right Twist (M1R)
Insert left needle from back to front under the horizontal loop between the last stitch worked and next stitch on left needle.

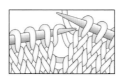

With right needle, knit into the front of this loop.

To make this increase on the purl side, insert left needle in same manner and purl into the front of the loop.

Decrease (Dec)

Knit 2 Together (K2tog)
Insert right needle through next two stitches on left needle as to knit. Knit these two stitches as one.

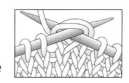
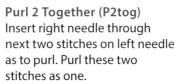

Purl 2 Together (P2tog)
Insert right needle through next two stitches on left needle as to purl. Purl these two stitches as one.

Slip, Slip, Knit (Ssk)
Slip next two stitches, one at a time, as to knit from left needle to right needle.

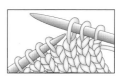

Insert left needle in front of both stitches and knit them together.

Slip, Slip, Purl (Ssp)
Slip next two stitches, one at a time, as to knit from left needle to right needle. Slip these stitches back onto left needle keeping them twisted. Purl these two stitches together through back loops.

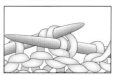

Two Stitches in One Stitch

Knit in Front & Back of Stitch (kfb)
Knit the next stitch in the usual manner, but don't remove the stitch from the left needle. Place right needle behind left needle

and knit again into the back of the same stitch. Slip original stitch off left needle.

Purl in Front & Back of Stitch (pfb)
Purl the next stitch in the usual manner, but don't remove the

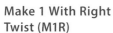

stitch from the left needle. Place right needle behind left needle and purl again into the back of the same stitch. Slip original stitch off left needle.

Pick Up & Knit
Step 1: With right side facing, working 1 st in from edge, insert tip of needle in space between first and second stitches.

Step 2: Wrap yarn around needle.

Step 3: Pull loop through to front.

Step 4: Repeat Steps 1–3.

Provisional Cast-On

Using waste yarn and crochet hook, make a chain a few sts more than the number of sts to be cast on. With knitting needle and project yarn, pick up and knit in back bump of each chain until required number of cast-on sts is on needle. When indicated in pattern, "unzip" the crochet chain to free live sts.

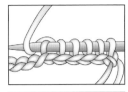

Binding off (knit)

Knit first two stitches on left needle. Insert tip of left needle into first stitch worked on right needle and pull it over the second stitch and completely off the needle.

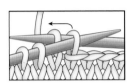

Knit the next stitch and repeat. When one stitch remains on right needle, cut yarn and draw tail through last stitch to fasten off.

Binding off (purl)

Purl first two stitches on left needle. Insert tip of left needle into first stitch worked on right needle and pull it over the second stitch and completely off the needle.

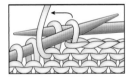

Purl the next stitch and repeat. When one stitch remains on right needle, cut yarn and draw tail through last stitch to fasten off.

Kitchener Stitch

This method of grafting live stitches together is often used for the toes of socks and flat seams. To graft edges together and form an uninterrupted piece of of stockinette stitch fabric, divide all stitches evenly onto two knitting needles—one behind the other. Thread yarn into tapestry needle. Hold needles with wrong sides together and work from right to left as follows:

Step 1:
Insert tapestry needle into first stitch on front needle as to purl. Draw yarn through stitch, leaving stitch on knitting needle.

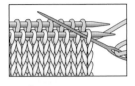

Step 2:
Insert tapestry needle into the first stitch on the back needle as to purl. Draw yarn through stitch and slip stitch off knitting needle.

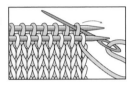

Step 3:
Insert tapestry needle into the next stitch on same (back) needle as to knit, leaving stitch on knitting needle.

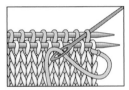

Step 4:
Insert tapestry needle into the first stitch on the front needle as to knit. Draw yarn through stitch and slip stitch off knitting needle.

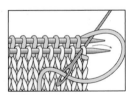

Step 5:
Insert tapestry needle into the next stitch on same (front) needle as to purl. Draw yarn through stitch, leaving stitch on knitting needle.

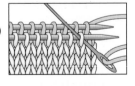

Repeat Steps 2 through 5 until one stitch is left on each needle. Then repeat Steps 2 and 4. Fasten off. Grafted stitches should be the same size as adjacent knitted stitches.

Meet the Designer

Tabetha Hedrick, a freelance knitwear designer and writer raising a family in Colorado, lives by the belief that joy comes when fully participating in the present moment. And that joy is ever so easy to find when immersed in the world of fiber!

Her work has been published in numerous digital and print magazines, books and yarn company pattern collections. Tabetha's indie patterns, portfolio, blog and teaching schedule can be found on her website: www.tabethahedrick.com.

Special Thanks

Special Thanks to Koigu Wool Designs for supplying all the wonderful yarn for this book. All projects were made using Koigu Painter's Palette Premium Merino (KPPPM) and/or Koigu Premium Merino (KPM).

KOIGU WOOL DESIGNS
Box 158
Chatsworth, ON N0H 1G0
CANADA
1(888)765-WOOL
www.koigu.com

Photo Index

A Playful Palette of 10 Knitted Accessories is published by Annie's, 306 East Parr Road, Berne, IN 46711. Printed in USA.
Copyright © 2013 Annie's. All rights reserved. This publication may not be reproduced in part or in whole without written permission from the publisher.

RETAIL STORES: If you would like to carry this pattern book or any other Annie's publications, visit AnniesWSL.com.

Every effort has been made to ensure that the instructions in this pattern book are complete and accurate. We cannot, however, take responsibility for human error, typographical mistakes or variations in individual work. Please visit AnniesCustomerCare.com to check for pattern updates.

978-1-59635-885-0

1 2 3 4 5 6 7 8 9